# Drum Circle
# Facilitators' Handbook

**Nellie Hill**     **Arthur Hull**

**Cover photo:** Thanks to REMO, Inc., for cover photo permission. In memoriam to Paulo Mattioli Dec 31,1969 - Oct 22, 2011.

Drum Circle Facilitators' Handbook

**Second Edition**

Village Music Circles
108 Coalinga Way,
Santa Cruz, CA 95060
USA

Phone: (831) 458-1946
Fax: (831) 459-7215

www.drumcircle.com
outreach@drumcircle.com

Printed in China

**Library of Congress Cataloging-in-Publication Data**

Hull, Arthur 1947-
Hill, Nellie 1949-
   Drum Circle Facilitators' Handbook/Arthur Hull and Nellie Hill
   Includes biographical references and index.
   **ISBN #: 978-0-9724307-4-6**
   1. Group rhythmic event facilitation–Instruction and study.
   2. Community music–Instruction and study.
   3. Percussion instruments–Instruction and study.
   4. Musical meter and rhythm–Instruction and study.

# Table of Contents

# About This Book

This book is for anyone who has the desire to facilitate rhythm-based events. This includes anyone entering the field of facilitated rhythm-based events, practicing facilitators, to trained graduates of Village Music Circles Playshops. This handbook will help you better serve almost any population or constituency ranging from family-friendly rhythm events, to kids in school, special needs populations, the well elderly, and corporate team-building events.

Our format takes you from the first call for booking a circle, to what things are helpful to know and how to set up for the function. It covers the basic structure of a great facilitated event from drum call to closing. There are questions for reflection and lots of places where you can write things that you find helpful to remember in your own circles. The book also includes many reference materials, concepts of drum facilitation, Arthur's triplicities, ideas for writing your own contract, etc. The back of the book has several pages for you to track your events and of course a place for you to write your ideas, discoveries, and learnings.

# Preface

Parents know they do not own their children. The children have been entrusted into their loving care to nurture and help them grow to their highest potential. Although they have lots of control in the beginning of the child's life cycle, children will still manage to explore the world and get into creative trouble while generating "learning moments" and life's lessons in their own special way. Slowly the parents release control as their children grow into adolescence. They try to educate them through example to make the right choices, mentoring them into adulthood. As they go their own way, parents trust their offspring will make the right decisions.

Similarly, you are the parent of any drum circle that you help birth, and you are responsible for mentoring it to its fullest potential. A drum circle is a living entity that has a life cycle of its own. It progresses from birth to adolescence, to maturity, and finally a celebratory completion.

A drum circle is a gestalt of many elements coming together to create *In-The-Moment* rhythmical alchemy between everyone involved. The type, age and intention of the people who attend a particular rhythm-based event determine how you will choose to facilitate their drum circle. Every drum circle event is different from any other, but there are some basics elements and patterns that appear in most rhythmical events.

Participants come into a drum circle as individuals, play their way into group consciousness, to evolve into an ensemble and ultimately play together as an orchestra. In this interactive gestalt, your job as facilitator changes as the group dynamic evolves. First you teach the body language you will use to facilitate. Then you direct the group's attention to the elements that will make their ensemble work well together. Finally, you facilitate the drum circle toward becoming a fully connected orchestra, with you as conductor.

A rhythm event that you are facilitating is your baby. With your help and guidance it will grow and mature into a sophisticated playing ensemble over a period of an hour or two. When you add the key element of *Sharing your Spirit* your event will be a success.

Nellie Hill and I designed this Drum Circle Facilitators' Handbook to help guide you along your journey. We offer questions for you to ask yourself, along with practical examples and hints. We hope these ideas will enhance your personal and professional development as a rhythm event facilitator—one drum circle at a time.

*Arthur Hull*

# Introduction

When I started out as a facilitator, I kept wishing for a concise manual to remind me of things I needed to do. I remember getting to a gig and finding out there were no chairs. I did a campfire without any lights (try facilitating with only a flashlight around your neck and a roaring fire at your back!). I did not know what to ask before the gig. This book will help you remember the little things.

It is also intended to be a refresher of the many things you can do within a circle. Sometimes we get into a rut and use the same techniques in every circle just because we have not thought about other options in a while. Here is a place where the basics are written down and you can also write in new ideas AND find them again.

Because my vision was to have something easy to carry and durable, this manual is 5x8 and printed on heavy weight bond.

Arthur and I put our heads together, grabbed the most essential skills represented in his two books, and came up with the format you see. It takes you from getting the gig to the final evaluation. Beside each set of skills are reminder questions to help you focus on what you need to be doing in every circle.

The back of the book supplies you with blank pages to take notes. It also includes Arthur's facilitation shorthand, what instruments are in a basic facilitator's kit, Arthur's triplicities, information about the Drum Circle Facilitators Guild, and more.

I hope this manual makes your job as a facilitator easier and more successful.

*Nellie Hill*

# Anatomy of a Rhythm-Based Event

The Anatomy of a Rhythm-Based Event chart represents the four basic phases that the facilitator and the participants experience as they create a successful, meaningful drum circle event. This book covers from beginning to end the phases represented on this chart.

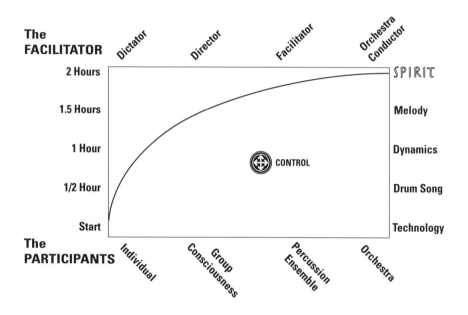

The line on the graph represents the change from facilitator management to participant control.

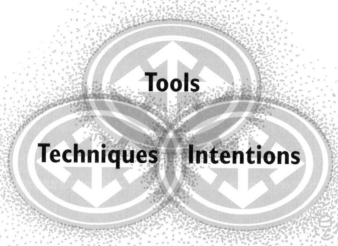

## Arthurian Facilitation
### Triplicity

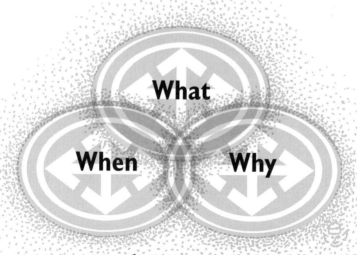

## Application of the
## Facilitation Triplicity

# Circle Preparations
## Purpose of the Circle

Before facilitating a circle there are a few things that you should think about.

What is the purpose or intent of the circle? What idea will be your focus? Is it just a gathering of friends or community? Is it celebrating something, remembering something or someone special? Is it to bring people together? Are there issues you should know about? Is there a theme or special topic?

It is a good idea to know as much as possible about your client before you do your circle. It will give you a sense of relationship with your participants if you care enough to know about what they do or who they are. Do your homework. Check their website. Ask lots of questions about who they are, what they expect, etc.

# Questions

**What do I know about the client? If a business, is there a mission statement?**

**Is there a theme for this event?**

**Is there a specific message that they want me to deliver?**

**How do I use the windows of communication between rhythms to convey the message of this event?**
- Thank the event organizer, participants
- Deliver short talking points
- Relate the activity of the rhythm to the purpose of the event

**Am I remembering to maintain a sense of humor?**

**Is the circle the only event or part of a bigger picture?**

**What is the dress code? How conservative do I need to be?**

# Things You Need to Know

In order to prepare for an event, you need to have a few basic facts:

- How many participants?
- Any handicapping conditions that need to be addressed? If so, what support staff will be available?
- Does the equipment need to be cleaned, for hospital or hospice?
- Is it a transient situation, open to the public, or a set population?
- Is it inside or outside? Day or night?
- If outside, is there a rain plan? Lighting? Canopy or tent? Shade?
- Are chairs supplied? Will chairs be set up for me?
- If more than one group, how much time for transitions?
- How much time for set up? Break down?
- If inside, what is the flexibility for set up? (Chairs and tables? Auditorium seating? Long ballroom?)
- What type and shape of room is it? (Conference room? Auditorium? School room?)
- What type of floor? (Carpet? Wood? Cement?)
- Is there a noise threshold or a nearby event?
- Is drinking water available?
- If planning to record the event, what kind of permission forms will be needed?
- Will alcohol be involved?
- Do I need a parking permit?

It is wise to check in with the event a few days before to make sure all is set, confirming date, time and location and any needed arrangements have been made.

# Answers To Essential Questions

Problems I need to solve:

**Are chairs provided? If not, source?**

**Is it in an accessible place?**

**Is it on the ground floor? If not, is there an elevator?**

**Where can I load and unload?**

**Will there be help?**

**Sound system? Electricity?**

**Time frame for cleaning up the room after your event?**

## Other Hints

All of the answers to these questions will help you be successful. The more you know, the less you have to deal with when you arrive and the more fun you can have.

Acoustic hint (with apologies to anyone with you when you walk into your venue): shout out a big "Hey!" and listen to the sound response that the room gives you. The sound feedback from your yell will help you place your circle in the room for the best acoustic effect.

Avoid placing your drum circle in the middle of a gymnasium. You will get four delayed echoes from four different directions. Putting the drum circle in a corner of the gym will give you better sound.

# NOTES

# OTHER QUESTIONS
# I HAVE ENCOUNTERED

# OTHER QUESTIONS
# I HAVE ENCOUNTERED

# Setting Up the Circle

## A Single Circle for 20 to 30 People

A setup for 20 to 30 people would be a single circle with shoulder to shoulder seating and 2 aisles to GOOW (Get Out Of the Way).

## Concentric Circles for More Than 30 People

Set up concentric circles with four aisles. The population sitting in concentric circles expands as you add more rows of chairs.

Example:

- First row: 16 chairs, 4 chairs between each of the four aisles. Total population, 16 people.
- Second row: 24 chairs with 6 chairs between each of the aisles. Total population, 40 people.
- Third row: 32 chairs with 8 chairs between each of the aisles. Total population, 72 people.

On the next page is a standard seating chart that Village Music Circles sends to their clients.

## Build a "Sound Bowl" for Small Spaces

For maximum players with minimum space:

- The first inside circle is populated with players seated on the floor with hand percussion and small drums.
- The second concentric circle has chairs with sit down drums (ashikos, congas, djembes).
- The third concentric circle is populated by standing players (drums on stands, straps, frame drums, etc.) Be sure to leave aisles!

## Remember to Save Yourself a Seat

If you love to drum as much as facilitate, save yourself a seat in the center seating ring of your circle. After a facilitation sequence you can sit down and play with the group. This will allow you have a place to enjoy the solid rhythmic foundation you've helped create, be a drummer for a little bit, and feel the circle the way your participants do.

# Seating Chart

## Chair Setup

There are usually 24 in the first, inside row.
Chairs are added to increase the size of outgoing circles to accommodate varying chair sizes and numbers of participants.
In this example for 104 the setup is 24 • 36 • 44
Aisles are placed in four directions.

*Village Music Circles*™

# Dealing With the Unknown

What do you do if you don't know exactly how many people are coming, but you are told to expect around a certain number.

Example:

You are told to expect "maybe" around 100 people at your event. If you set up a 100 person chair drum circle, you may only have 60 people come. As the back rows fill up with the "just curious" players or timid participants, and the front rows fill up with the excited participants, you will have big holes of empty seats in your drum circle orchestra pit.

Solution:

If you expect to get 100 participants at your event but are not sure of the numbers, set up a three-row drum circle for 72 players, similar to the concentric circles setup listed on the previous page.

Then set up 3 or 4 stacks of chairs in strategic places outside the circle. When most of the original seating is filled, add more chairs and start to build a fourth row of participants.

The hardest part is getting people to come to the center circle first! Either wearing your drum or playing a bell or block, greet your guests as they arrive, encourage them to come forward and play with you. If you are lucky enough to have a greeter, make sure they are sending participants to the front first.

# THINGS I NEED TO REMEMBER TO BRING TO MY GIGS

# Drum/Percussion Mix

A good drum/percussion mix for a circle is 1/2 drums, 1/2 percussion or, in some situations, 1/3 drums and 2/3 percussion.

It helps to set out the instruments in advance if possible.

Low drums are best placed in the center circle to help maintain the beat.

Aside from placing all (or most) of the low drums in the center, most drum circle setups would be: A drum in one seat, a bell in the next, then another type of drum in the next chair, a shaker in the next chair, a drum in the next, a wood block in the next and so on.

It is good to have extra instruments set up on a table or in a container near the entrance for late-comers. The greeter should be there to make sure they have something to play and for added security.

# What I Need

**What instrument mix do I need for this group?**

**Where is the door?**
Set up my "Playing chair" in the center row where I can see people coming in.

**Did I leave aisle ways to "get out of the way" (GOOW)?**

**Do I have a seat in the circle so that I can join the circle after I facilitate?**

**Are instruments accessible to newcomers to the circle?**

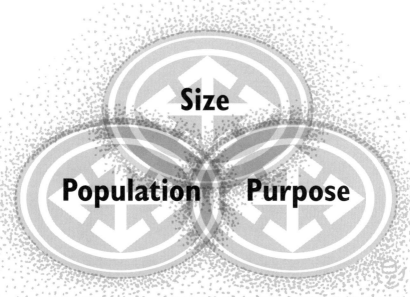

# Drum Circle Format
## Triplicity

# Drum Call

Drum Call is the foundation of the entire event. No matter how short or long, it initiates the relationship and builds rapport. It is where you teach your body language for basic facilitation, volume up-down, speed up, stop, continue to play, etc.

How your participants first see you sets the tone of the entire event. Make sure your attire fits the event. Business casual is almost always appropriate. A tee shirt and torn jeans will not win over your participants and does not present you as a professional.

A big smile and good eye contact goes a long way to putting everyone at ease. Letting them know that there are no wrong notes just different ones gives them the confidence to participate fully. Be willing to be flexible with your setup to insure that everyone is comfortable.

Be ready to set the beat, and help the groove to solidify. Make sure everyone can see you and read your signals.

Here are some of the basic tools or techniques you would use in DRUM CALL.

### Attention Call

Step into the center with your hand in the air and walk around the center until you have everyone's attention.

### Tempo Attention

Instead of an open hand, use a raised and lowered arm cue signal. Remember that you ARE allowed to tell them what you are going to do!

### Volume Attention

Place hands facing up about waist high and raise arms to indicate volume up, hands facing down and lowering arms for volume down.

### Call and Response

Hold up whatever instrument you will be using to give the call. Point to it and then to the circle several times, then play your call. It is OK to say something like "I Play - You Play."

### Rumble

This is an action that initiates and controls rhythm chaos. Hold hands in front and wiggle quickly from the wrists. A rumble can be used as a transition point or as something inside an ongoing rhythm. It can also be used as an opening, a closing, or as a showcase tool.

### Stop Cut

Give an attention call first, then give a definitive signal to stop. Stop cut motion is bringing the hands up to an X across the chest and then quickly releasing the X, on the beat, with hands out to the side. You must be secure.

## Call to Groove

"1, 2, everybody play," "1, 2, start your groove," or "1, 2, here we go."

Be sure to keep a pulse in your voice, phraseology and body.

## Accent Note

Different than a stop cut, the accent note is facilitated by a sharp downward whole body motion. The easiest way to start is to use single accents on the pulses or simple patterns. Do a stop cut. Then a swift downward motion to play, then again, maybe 2 or 3 accents or more.

After you have demonstrated this, then you can add accents during the groove while the group is continuing to play.

With these basic facilitating skills, you have established rapport and are moving the group to the next step: facilitating to group consciousness.

# The Seven Elements of Drum Call

**1. Take Responsibility for the Physical Circle.**
Take charge of seating and instrument arrangement.

**2. Teach Your Facilitator Body Language.**
Teach the body language signals for the basic facilitation directions.

**3. Define the Roles.**
By your actions and words you verbally define your role as facilitator and their roles as contributing players.

**4. Establish Trust.**
Trust is the seed that you plant at the beginning of the program and nurture throughout the event.

**5. Teach Without Teaching.**
Use *Experiential Training* by facilitating musical examples that educate the players about the makeup of the orchestra that they will become.

**6. Orchestrate Self-Facilitation.**
Orchestrate the group's ability to facilitate its own musical interaction and cooperation.

**7. Read the Group.**
Constantly develop your Facilitator's Radar. Read and evaluate the *In-The-Moment* music-making situation on all levels.

For a deeper understanding of these concepts as well as the tri-plicities, refer to *Drum Circle Facilitation, Building Community Through Rhythm.*

# Questions

How long will I have for drum call? When do I know it is over or time to move on?

Are my facilitation calls clear and precise?

Can I feel the pulse? If not, what should I be doing, or facilitating, to help the group generate it? (Dance a little bit in the circle? Play the pulse in the air with my stick or on a bell?)

Is everyone participating? How can I help engage them?
- Exchange instruments?
- Change seats?
- Rhythm Dynamics?

What rhythm games do I have in my bag to help if needed?

# Rhythm Game Ideas

The rhythm games below are two of the thirty-one games that can be found in Arthur's book, *Rhythmical Alchemy Playshop, Volume 1, Drum Circle Games.*

## Layering in a Rhythm

Layering in a Rhythm is a basic groove starter that invites the participants to synchronize and synergize their playing.

### Play the Game

- Designate a starting player. While no one is playing, that person starts the rhythm song.
- The person to the left of the starting player listens to the rhythm and then adds whatever rhythm they think would be appropriate to support and harmonize with the song being played.
- The person to the left of the second player listens to the two players, and then adds their complementary rhythm.
- The next person in turn listens to the song being created and plays their rhythmical contribution.
- This process continues until each player in the circle has layered their complementary part into the composition, creating a complete rhythm song.
- After everyone joins the rhythm and enjoys the composition for a while, the person who started the rhythm makes an attention call, shouts "Rumble!" and leads the groove to a close.
- The next volunteer starts a rhythm and continues this game. With a small group, you can take turns until everyone has had a chance to start a rhythm. No two songs will be the same.

# Groove By the Numbers, Beginner Version

The beginner version of Groove by the Numbers teaches players how to place their notes as a contribution into a group rhythm, as they listen to the spaces between the other notes being played. Drummers choose between a tone, a slap, and a bass note. Hand percussion instrument players may choose a bell, shaker, or wood block, and their sound can be a ding, a shush or a doink.

## Play the Game

- Participants choose their number.
- The game facilitator counts aloud from one to eight in cycles, while playing the one & the five on the bell.
- After the first cycle of counting, everyone in the drum circle plays on the number that they chose. As the count continues, players strike their instruments each time their number is called, and they continue playing that foundation note throughout the piece.
- The facilitator continues to count and play the bell on the one and the five until every player has joined the groove.
- Once the rhythm song solidifies, the facilitator stops counting aloud, de-emphasizing the numbers, so players focus on their musical relationship to the song.
- After a few more cycles, the facilitator stops marking the pulse with the bell.
- The facilitator invites players to improvise by embellishing their rhythm song with a few more notes.
- The facilitator joins the group, playing to complement and solidify the group's groove.

For beginners and younger kids, count slowly at first and then increase the tempo gradually as the groove solidifies.

# OTHER POSSIBLE GAMES

# Questions

Do I have the tools in the center of the circle to help me sculpt? (wood block, bell, shaker, big white stick)

As I walk around the outside of the circle, am I listening for the different drum/percussion songs I can showcase?

What songs do I hear that I can help support, strengthen or use to assist the group of players progress to a more sophisticated, interactive musicality?

Is there a group I need to highlight or pay extra attention to?

Is the low drum song balanced and serving as a foundation to support the rest of the players?

# Sculpting

## Sculpt by Timbre

Identify all the people playing a specific timbre: shakers, bells, woods, drums. This is easily done by holding up an example of what you want and pointing to it, giving a continue to play signal at the instrument type. Stop cut the remainder of the circle (ROC), listen for a few cycles and call everyone back to groove.

You can carry this further by doing more than one timbre, or layering in by type (starting with the shakers, adding metal, then wood, then drums).

## Sculpt by Drum Pitch

This can be either low, medium, or high pitch. It is always good to introduce the sound of the lowest drums so everyone tunes into the beat. It also allows the circle to actually hear the many different tonalities of the drums.

Usually you do not have many low drums so it is easy to sculpt. High drums are also distinctive.

## Sculpt by Drum Type or Drum Pitch

You can sculpt and showcase one type of drum being played. Some examples are dunduns, ashikos, congas, djembes, or frame drums.

After you have showcased the different types of drums, you can then easily group them by pitch types, enabling each participant to know a little more about his instrument and the different tonalities of each drum type. Again your groupings would be low, medium and high.

# Questions

Am I aware of how often I am going into the center of the circle?
Am I letting the rhythm last long enough before I intervene?

Am I being careful about listening to the needs of the group, not my agenda?

How far apart are the musical/rhythmical transitions?

Am I staying out of the circle, or sitting down and playing with it, more than I am going into the center to facilitate?

Am I letting the transitions develop so that I get more information about how to facilitate the group before I intervene?

## Sculpt by Gender

This is showcasing either all the men or all the women of the group. Some people have found it is most effective to just hold up a sign designating which gender they want to sculpt. The end result is a very different sound from each group.

## Half Circle Sculpts

Half circle sculpts are foundational techniques that, when used with a simple call and response or rumbles, are a teaching without teaching technique. They educate the players to pay attention and respond to the whole circle rather than just the people around them.

## Sculpt by Concentric Circle

Showcasing each ring or row of players in your drum circle creates another layer of sound. It allows the front row to actually hear what is going on behind them!

# Questions

Am I now helping to guide them to where they want to go, or am I still totally in control?

Do I recognize when the group is moving towards orchestration consciousness?

What do I still need to do to take them to orchestration consciousness?

Are there any facilitation activities that I have already done that I should repeat to solidify the group's progression towards orchestration?

# NOTES

# NOTES

Sound
Orchestration

Rhythmical
& Playing
Expertise

Group
Consciousness

Drum Circle Potential
Triplicity

# Facilitation Towards Orchestration Consciousness

Now the members of the circle are interacting with each other with an understanding of percussion ensemble consciousness. You may now become a facilitator and guide the group towards its highest musical potential, orchestration consciousness.

You can move the group towards musical dialogue, rhythmical dialogue and musical phrasing, harmony and dynamics.

You do this by sculpting drum/percussion songs with mixed timbres and pitches. Also you can sculpt the circle of players for more sophisticated musical interaction.

# Sculpt by Sections

Clearly mark the section you want to play by extending your hand and slice as if you were cutting out a piece of pie from the center. Then hold that hand in place and use the other hand to sweep until you have marked where you want the section to end. Eye contact is essential.

This simple sculpt is your ticket to so many other different facilitation actions. Anything you do with your sculpted group will usually be an active facilitation.

Some examples of facilitation actions are volume changes, accent notes, call and response.

The circle can be in halves, thirds or quarters. Each additional sculpting gives you the opportunity for a higher level of facilitation.

# Sculpt a Song

Select a variety of players whose musical contributions go very well together. Ask them to keep playing both verbally and by signal. The first time you do this it helps to verbally reinforce that they are to keep playing no matter what you tell the rest of the group to do.

When you stop cut the rest of the group, let the song go a few cycles and then bring the players back to the groove.

HINT: The type of song that you are showcasing should represent the basic elements of music making, such as interactive rhythm, dialogue, and melody line.

# Questions

Am I remembering to keep it simple to start?

Am I careful not to sculpt the same sections every time?

When selecting a song, am I choosing players by using an inviting open hand instead of pointing at them with a finger?

Am I making clear eye contact? Smiling?

When I bring the rest of the players back into the ongoing rhythm groove, am I remembering to acknowledge my showcased players?

# Sculpt Using
# Vocal or Body Percussion

Create a platform by sculpting and showcasing a timbre (shakers?) that will support vocal or body percussion. Or you can bring down the volume of the whole circle.

On top of this platform you can add improvisational percussive sounds, a song or chants. There are many ways you can easily go from non-instruments back to instrumentation.

# Using Volume for Consciousness

After creating a platform, bring the volume down to very soft then highlight special sounds, patterns (etc.) that have appeared in the circle. This allows the group to become more aware of the musicality around them. Layering in percussion or drum pitch would create a subtle transition to volume consciousness. A call to groove would be a dynamic transition to full groove.

# Questions

When doing vocals, can I include the purpose of the circle?

Am I aware of the decibel level (volume) of the group?

Do I make an effort to vary the volume, making a more dynamic musical circle?

# NOTES

# NOTES

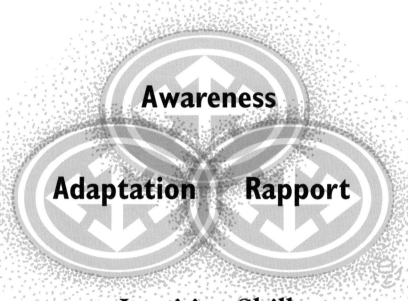

# Intuitive Skills
## Triplicity

# Orchestrating the Circle

You know the group is in full orchestration consciousness when they no longer need you. There are no transition points to call you in to facilitate. In adult, family friendly, recreational circles, you have established a trusting relationship with the group where they want you to step into the center and orchestrate their music making. With their permission, you orchestrate their music by applying the concepts laid out in this book and the book *Drum Circle Facilitation*.

Your drum circle is in orchestration consciousness when the group of players are fully engaged in listening and supporting each other in an evolving *In-The-Moment* musical project in which they have ownership.

At this point in the circle's evolution, you are stepping into the orchestration spot to help bring out the melody line and the musicality of the group's collaboration. You have given the circle participants the tools that they need to play together, and have shown the many possibilities of drum songs when played with dynamics.

Now that the group is self-facilitating, you can step in with your ears fully tuned to the musical possibilities. The circle is in full listening mode and the fun continues to the next level. Here are just a few ideas that can help move things along.

# Sculpting a Song, Next Level

As a facilitator, you will be selecting a mixture of timbres and pitches in the group with a specific purpose in mind. The purpose is to create an example of a group of people who are listening to each other, creating a musical dialogue, thereby creating a harmonic melody line.

This gives the entire group a real-time model of what they are aspiring to. When you bring the group back to groove, they are playing to that example, which improves the musicality of the entire group. Each time you sculpt a song, it raises their musical consciousness.

It is also good to allow the members of the group to come in when they are ready, "at your leisure." This allows the participants to take the time to listen to the song being played and figure out what would fit best with that song. They become very conscious of what they contribute to the song and how the song has changed because of their input. This is a perfect way to develop orchestration consciousness!

# Questions

What am I listening for, to take the circle to orchestration consciousness?

Am I being careful not to step in until I am needed?

Am I aware of *all* the participants? Is anyone being left out? Is anyone struggling or not playing?

# NOTES

# Building a Platform

Sculpting out a section — a song or timbre to continue playing — constitutes a musical/rhythmical platform. Stop the remainder of the playing group. Then over the platform you can create other musical activities, either with rumbles, accents, call and response, vocals, etc.

Make sure your platform is secure before you attempt to do something over it. This is especially important when you select and sculpt a specific song to continue.

Half, third and quarter section sculpts are fairly common.

By sculpting out a platform, you can layer in and out different groups of players.

Use the players in a platform to bring out your soloists to allow them to shine.

# Teeter-Totter

Divide the group in half. Bring the volume down on one side while doing volume up on the other. Then reverse the volumes for a teeter-totter. Repeat several times.

Do this slowly at first. Then decrease the length of time each side is loud or soft. Then increase the teeter-totter volume change faster towards a new exciting tempo. We call this action *modulation*.

Tempo up or down is sometimes needed to move the groove along.

# Sculpting by Pitch

You can also sculpt by pitch. First the participants must know whether they are playing a low, medium or high instrument. Once pitch groups are identified, you can create a song by mixing the three pitches in any order. One way to do this is by placing your hands at different heights to indicate different pitch groups.

Low pitched instruments would be played when your hands are at your knees. High pitches would be played when your hands are above your head. Medium pitches would be indicated with your hands at your waist. It is fun to combine them.

A variety of pitch sculpting games can be found in Arthur's book *Rhythmical Alchemy Playshop Volume 1, Drum Circle Games.*

# Questions

Am I being careful not to leave any group of players out of the music for too long?

Am I listening to the group? Are they listening to each other?

Where is the strongest sound connection? Can these players be my next sculpted platform?

At what point should the group come back together in full groove?

# Sequencing

Create a sequence of events that can help the groove. For example when in transition, a set of rumbles, to rumble accents, to accent patterns, to pulse, to groove is a sequence.

Here is an example of a sophisticated rhythm sequence.

## Rhythm Switch

Identify and layer out 3 or 4 sections, down to one section still playing. Warn the non-playing section next to the playing section, that they will begin playing on your signal when you stop the other group. With this new body language you will be able to switch the groove from one section to another on the same beat. Throw the groove to each section, in turn. Then bring back the sections to the groove until everyone is playing. You can also modulate the rhythm switch change faster towards a new exciting tempo.

Create small successes by always using your radar.

Use your ears. Sometimes the best orchestration is found by sculpting something inside the groove that can take the group to new musical dimensions. It might be a conversation between two or three players that you would like to highlight.

*"Follow the people following you,*
*Work with what they give you,*
*There are no mistakes."*

From the book *Drum Circle Facilitation*

# Questions

**Do I recognize when the group no longer needs me in the center of the circle?**

You might as well sit down and play with the circle!

**Am I always listening for that special moment that will take the circle to an even higher level of consciousness and musicality?**

# OTHER QUESTIONS
# I HAVE ENCOUNTERED

# Closing the Circle

Be aware of the time. Ask someone to keep track for you. Ask for at least a 5 to 10 minute warning before time to close the event. This will allow you the time you need to guide the group to a successful musical/emotional end.

Every circle needs to come to an end and we need to be careful how we close. The emotional context of the group determines how to bring them to close.

The intention of a facilitated closing sequence of events is to create an emotional sense of completion in your playing group.

Popular endings include tempo up to a grand rumble, stop cut with a few accents and a thank you.

Also the reverse, a gradual slowing of the tempo and/or decrease in volume until it is silent, a deep breath, a thank you and goodbye.

Layering out is also very effective. You simply sculpt out each timbre until you are left with chimes, frogs, shakers, or whatever you wish.

Layer out loudest to softest, or layer out players in sequence also works.

Always remember that the circle has given you a gift. Thank them for coming.

As your participants are leaving the event try to be at the exit to thank them for sharing their rhythmical spirit.

There is nothing wrong with asking for help gathering your instruments. It gives you a chance to chat with the participants and gives them a chance to get grounded again before leaving.

**Objective
Witness**

**Circle
Witness**

**Personal
Witness**

# Critique Technique
## Triplicity

# Evaluation

After the circle has closed, it is a good idea to evaluate what you did, what you loved and what you could improve. If possible, get feedback from both the participants and the organizer. A nice touch is a follow-up note to the person who booked the circle thanking them for the invitation.

For your self-evaluation, the basic Village Music Circles "Critique Technique" will give lots of information to help improve your performance as a facilitator and your group's performance as a drum circle.

Objective witness: "What Happened?"

Circle witness: "What worked & What needs work?"

Personal witness: "What would I do differently the next time to achieve a better result?"

Another way to get feedback is the participant evaluation form. Keep it very simple with either a rating scale of 1-5 or simple answer to your questions. Be sure to supply something to write with and provide a collection box.

On the next page is an example of a participant evaluation sheet that you can use, with our thanks and with permission from Jon at Peak Rhythms.

## Participant Evaluation Questions:

Overall I thought the rhythm event was:

_____

Specific things I enjoyed, learned or realized:

_____

_____

One thing I would recommend you add or change:

_____

## Comments:

_____

_____

## Optional:

Name _____

Date of Program _____

Position _____

_____ Permission to use my name and comments

*From Jon at Peak Rhythms, www.peakrhythms.com*

# MY SURVEY QUESTIONS

# The End and the Beginning

We wrote this handbook as a work in progress. The layout is set up so you can take notes and add what you personally need to help make you even more successful. It is a supplement for learning how to learn, a guide and a tool for moving you to your highest potential as a facilitator.

Every circle should be a learning environment for both you and your participants. As a facilitator, you are always striving to reach the highest level of musical collaboration in the circle.

Facilitate on the edge of your experience and knowledge. Then use this handbook to write new ideas, questions you need to remember, and great things you learn or see. The space is there for you to make it your handbook.

All we did was compile the basic skills in a concise format for reference. We want your feedback on this workbook. What can we do to make it even better for you? What did we leave out that you feel needs to be here? Let us know by emailing us:

Arthur Hull    arthurian@drumcircle.com
Nellie Hill    playfulspirit@mac.com

As of this printing we would like to thank the following for their support and contributions to this handbook: Jonathan Murray, Steve Hirsh, Jon Crowder, Steve Hill, Dennis Maberry, Scott Swimmer, Sam Rogers, Tom Tom Tomoko Yokota, Jessica Fredicks, Dick Marcus, Cameron Tummel, Otha Day, Simon Faulkner, Louis-Daniel Joly, David Chiller, Phyllis Mueller, Laurie Precht, and Cornell Cooley.

# Appendix

## Appendix I:
## Arthur's Facilitation Concepts

Facilitation Concepts help guide your actions in the circle. By putting these concepts to use it will make your job as a facilitator much easier and the success of your participants higher.

### What Can I Do to Serve This Circle?

Facilitation is a service-oriented art form. It is the mantra that will help keep your intentions on track as you juggle all the elements that surround you in a rhythm-based event. Drum circle facilitation is an act of service to the players, not a performance art. "What Can I Do to Serve the Circle" helps keep you in the moment.

### Create Small Successes

Creating simple successful rhythmical experiences for the players in the circle is a powerful way to educate the group and improve individual self-esteem. Facilitating several of these successes will guide the group toward maturing as a percussion ensemble. What is good for the circle is also good for you as the facilitator. Creating these small successes can create positive learning experiences for you as the facilitator, fine tune your skills, tools, and radar, and your confidence as a facilitator.

### Work With What They Give You

You, the facilitator, are only one of the many people in the circle. The ability to adapt and be flexible to the never-ending surprises that appear in a rhythm event is a sign of a maturing facilitator. Understand that you are all collaborating to create an *In-The-Moment* musical experience. Understanding that and keeping your heart open and your radar fully on will help you stay in the moment to receive the wonderful gifts they give you.

## Respect and Use the Transition Points

An essential concept of Arthurian-style facilitation is recognizing, respecting, and using the rhythmical transition points of your circle. A transition point is an invitation by the players to you as the facilitator to step into the orchestration spot to help guide the group's music to the next rhythm or to a successful conclusion. By listening to the group you can understand their playing consciousness and their level of rhythmical connection and you are ready to step in to guide them to the next level.

## Get Out of Their Way (GOOW)

Your role as a facilitator is no more and no less important than each player in your circle. The better you are at facilitating the group toward playing their own music, the less you need to facilitate. GOOW is exactly what you need to do when you have no reason to be in the orchestration spot. In Arthurian facilitation, if the group's music and rhythm are good and there is no transition point, then the players don't need your facilitation skill. What should you do? Sit down and play or step out of the circle and GOOW!

## Constantly Use Your Radar

To properly read the circle, you want to develop and use your peripheral sensibilities. The three peripheral reading tools: vision, hearing, and feeling, function together as your radar. A well balanced radar gives you all the information you need to best serve your group.

## There Are NO Mistakes

There are no mistakes, only opportunities for learning. You can apply this concept to the participants in your circle and to yourself as a facilitator. See those "mistakes" as learning opportunities for you as a facilitator in training.

# Important Questions

You can explore the Arthurian Facilitation Concepts in more detail in Chapter 5, page 91, in the book *Drum Circle Facilitation, Building Community through Rhythm.*

What can I do to serve this circle?
What kind of "be here now" mantra can I use that will work for me?

What can I do to make each facilitation step a small evolutionary learning experience?
How can I create many small successes?
Am I being careful to start with one step at a time?

Am I careful to work with what the circle gives me?
Is my radar tuned into those special elements that suddenly appear?

Am I respecting the transition points?
Do I recognize when the group is in full groove, fully engaged, and steady?

After facilitating a great sequence and the group is connected and steady, what do I do now?
GET OUT OF THEIR WAY!!!!!


Am I constantly using my radar?
Am I always aware to the information coming from the side or behind me?

# Appendix II: Basic Facilitator Kit

Variety of sound is the key to success in your drum kit when you are providing the equipment.

In the kit described below we are using 50% drums & 50% percussion, with equal amounts of low, medium, and high pitched drums and equal amounts of bell, shaker, and wood percussion timbre sounds.

Even in the same pitch or timbre group, you want to have a variety of instruments. Below are some examples.

## Drums
- **Low:** double-headed dun duns or surdos, Cuban tumbas, large frame drums
- **Medium:** Cuban congas, ashikos, REMO tubanos, medium frame drums
- **High:** bongos, djembes, talking drums, small frame drums

## Percussion
- **Bells:** agogo bells, cow bells, gankoguis
- **Shakers:** cylinder shakers, maracas, shekeres, tambourines
- **Wood:** recko-scrapers, wood blocks, claves

# Appendix III: Arthurian Triplicities

The following triplicities are the essence of facilitation. Each part of a triplicity has an impact on the other two parts, and without all three parts functioning equally, your circle has a weak link.

The first triplicity is Circle Facilitation Mastery. A great facilitator is not just a technician, but must also be sensitive to the participants and understand when the circle has reached its own musicality. All of the triplicities that follow this define what is facilitation, presence, and musicality.

By studying each section, you will have a deeper understanding of all the pieces involved in a successful circle.

# FACILITATION MASTERY

**Circle Facilitation**

**Musicality**    **Presence**

Special Thanks to Mary Tolena and Jim Boneau for contributing this Triplicity.

---

# CIRCLE FACILITATION
## Triplicity Group

**Vocal Skills**

**Group Leadership**    **Body Language**

### Presentation Skills
Triplicity

**Readability**

**Telegraph**    **Congruency**

### Body Language
Triplicity

**Visual**

**Auditory**    **Kinesthetic**

### Radar
Triplicity

**Size**

**Population**    **Purpose**

### Drum Circle Format
Triplicity

# PRESENCE
## Triplicity Group

**Rhythmical Empowerment**

**Community Building** · **Health & Wellness**

Intention
Triplicity

**Honesty**

**Rapport** · **Congruency**

Trust
Triplicity

**Awareness**

**Adaptation** · **Rapport**

Intuitive Skills
Triplicity

**Share your Rhythmical Bliss**

**Serve your Community** · **Develop Business Skills**

Career Development
Triplicity

 drumcircle.com

# MUSICALITY
## Triplicity Group

**Wood**

**Bells** · **Shakers**

Percussion Timbre
Triplicity

**Low Pitch**

**Medium Pitch** · **High Pitch**

Drum Pitch
Triplicity

**Sound Orchestration**

**Rhythmical & Playing Expertise** · **Group Consciousness**

Drum Circle Potential
Triplicity

**Universal Pattern**

**Interactive Rhythm** · **Melody Line**

Drum Circle Song
Triplicity

# Appendix IV: Making a Contract

## Things That Should Be in a Contract

Every facilitator needs some form of contract or letter of agreement in order to solidify what is expected from you and your client. Here are suggestions as to what to include:

- Location, date and time
- Compensation
- When payment is due (if there is a retainer, and when it is due) and who to make payment to
- Cancellation policy, theirs and yours
- Description of performance, including what you are providing, and how many participants you are expecting
- Damage policy
- Travel arrangements, including accommodations

## Expectations of the Client

- What equipment they are providing, including chairs, sound system, lighting, canopies, etc.
- Parking arrangements, preferably near loading site, permits, etc.
- Is client providing assistance, security, hotel staff?
- Contact person
- Hiring organization
- If out of town, is the client covering transportation and equipment costs?

## Pricing

There are so many factors that help determine your fee. Only you can decide what works for you.

- Experience (professional, intermediate, beginner)
- Client (profit, non-profit, corporate)
- Geography
- Size of event
- Type of event (party, team building, health and wellness)

# Appendix V:
# Drum Circle Facilitators Guild

The Drum Circle Facilitators Guild (DCFG) is a professional organization for drum circle facilitators. Guild members are dedicated to serving communities through rhythm-based events designed to empower, unite, and promote well being. Facilitators routinely work in health care, education, professional and community settings.

The guild supports the individuals who serve unique populations where drum circles are used as a beneficial tool for facilitating wellness, community and creative expression.

Founded in 2001 in Washington, D.C., the DCFG was established by a group of professional facilitators as a 501c(6) non-profit organization. This global organization includes members from the United States, Canada, the United Kingdom, and Japan, among others.

As a professional association, DCFG supports its members through education, marketing, and accreditation.

The DCFG website showcases and markets guild members, outlining their experience, education and clientele. It also acts as a resource of information for professional DCF's, providing networking opportunities, resources, and business tools.

One of the most significant services of the guild is putting on a three-day international conference every year. This conference includes presentations on business practices, education, new products and health and wellness.

**For more information or to join please visit: www.dcfg.net**

# Appendix VI: Facilitator Shorthand

This section provides a system of shorthand you can use to write in your log exactly what you did every time you stepped into the circle. By doing this you will better understand not only what you did, how often you stepped in, but the what and why of your facilitation.

Many thanks to Jonathan Murray for developing this system.

## Shorthand Notation ACTIONS

| | | | |
|---|---|---|---|
| + | Start of Sequence | (ear) | Listening |
| ↻ | Call to Groove | /// | Layering In |
| → | Group in Groove | \\\ | Layering Out |
| G | Continue to Play | ✓ | Accent Downbeats |
| ! | Attention Call | ↗ | Volume Up |
| ⊗ | Stop Cut | ↘ | Volume Down |
| ∿ | Rumble | ↑ | Speed Up Tempo |
| ↵ | Call and Response | ↓ | Slow Down Tempo |
| ∅ | Sculpt | ✩ | Showcase |
| ⊖ | 1/2 Circle Sculpt | △ | Pass Out Part |
| ⊕ | 1/4 Circle Sculpt | ↗↘ | Teeter Totter |
| ⊘ | 1/3 Circle Sculpt | ↩↘ | Switchback |
| ♪ | Clap | ∿∿ | Modulation |
| | | ∫ | Wave |

# Shorthand Notation THINGS

O  Whole Circle

⊓  Platform

V  Vocal

♂  Men

♀  Women

K  Children

ROC  Rest of the Circle

P  Percussion

B  Bell

S  Shaker

W  Wood

T  Tambourine

Bw  Boomwhackers

◎  Window of Communication

D  Drums

L  Low Pitch

M  Medium Pitch

H  High Pitch

A  Ashiko

C  Conga

Dn  Dunnun

Dj  Djembe

Dk  Doumbek

F  Frame Drum

Ss  Sound Shape

# Appendix VII: DC Facilitator's Log

Every event that you facilitate is a learning experience. It is wise to sit down as soon as possible after you have facilitated a drum circle and recall the events and learning moments that have just taken place.

Writing down answers to the Critique Technique Triplicity questions and reading the Evaluation section on pages 60 & 61 will help turn your experience into action strategies that will constantly improve your radar and your facilitation skills. Writing down your thoughts, impressions and biggest learnings in a DCFacilitator's Log will help solidify your learning moments from that event.

As a part of the Village Music Circles Certification process, advance Mentor graduates are required to maintain and submit a DCFacilitator's Log. Many of those who had not kept a Facilitator's Log prior to their certification assignments continued to make entries into their Logs long after their assignments were complete.

On the following pages you will find a simple outline for taking notes after each event that you facilitate. These note pages are what constitute a basic DCFacilitator's Log book.

Use the DCFacilitator's Log pages and see what wonderful learning surprises you can glean from reviewing and critiquing your drum circles.

Feel free to copy the log pages, enlarge them and create your own DCFacilitator's Log Book.

# DRUM CIRCLE FACILITATOR'S LOG

Date _____ Place _____

Purpose of Event _____

Type of Venue _____

Number of Participants_____ Age Range _____

Special considerations _____

Sequence of the Events:

# DRUM CIRCLE FACILITATOR'S LOG

Date _____ Place _____

Purpose of Event _____

Type of Venue _____

Number of Participants_____ Age Range _____

Special considerations _____

Sequence of the Events:

# DRUM CIRCLE FACILITATOR'S LOG

Date _____ Place _____

Purpose of Event _____

Type of Venue _____

Number of Participants_____ Age Range _____

Special considerations _____

Sequence of the Events:

# DRUM CIRCLE FACILITATOR'S LOG

Date _____ Place _____

Purpose of Event _____

Type of Venue _____

Number of Participants_____ Age Range _____

Special considerations _____

Sequence of the Events:

# DRUM CIRCLE FACILITATOR'S LOG

Date _____ Place _____

Purpose of Event _____

Type of Venue _____

Number of Participants_____ Age Range _____

Special considerations _____

Sequence of the Events:

# DRUM CIRCLE FACILITATOR'S LOG

Date _____ Place _____

Purpose of Event _____

Type of Venue _____

Number of Participants_____ Age Range _____

Special considerations _____

Sequence of the Events:

# DRUM CIRCLE FACILITATOR'S LOG

Date _____ Place_____

Purpose of Event _____

Type of Venue _____

Number of Participants_____ Age Range _____

Special considerations _____

Sequence of the Events:

# Biographies

 **Nellie Hill,** Playful Spirit Adventures, is a Remo endorsed professional Drum Circle Facilitator. Her extensive facilitator training includes Village Music Circles certification. Other facilitation trainings include mentoring at VMC Hawaii and HealthRhythms including the Adolescent Protocol. She has her MA in Music Education from the University of Maryland, with extensive post graduate studies at Duquesne and Villanova Universities. Nellie has been a very active member of the Drum Circle Facilitators Guild, serving in all officer positions including President. She is still very much involved in this organization.

Ms. Hill has extensive experience in facilitating a variety of events. She facilitated the opening of the National Music Center, presented at the 2009 Music Educators National Conference in Washington, D.C., and conducted workshops for Peabody University and National Geographic. She has led teacher workshops in many counties in both Maryland and Virginia. She loves to do school residencies where the students have the opportunity to experience playing instruments from all over the world. Making music together is not only fun but builds community and understanding.

You may contact her at:
playfulspirit@mac.com
www.playfulspiritadventures.com

 Often referred to as the father of the modern facilitated drum circle, **Arthur Hull** is a recognized pioneer and Elder in what is now called the facilitated recreational drum movement. A gifted rhythmatist and charismatic facilitator, Arthur leads diverse groups through joyful and inspiring experiences using music and rhythm. His wit and humor motivate people beyond the cultural and personal barriers and he inspires enthusiastic participation.

Since 1990 Arthur has provided professional rhythm event facilitation trainings for community drum circle facilitators, educators, musicians, and corporate trainers. He has trained over nine thousand facilitators in over twenty countries.

Arthur wrote the first drum facilitation book *Drum Circle Spirit - Facilitating Human Potential Through Rhythm* in 1998. His second book *Drum Circle Facilitation - Building Community Through Rhythm* was published in 2006. He also recorded an accompanying DVD *Drum Circle Facilitation - Building Community Through Rhythm.*

His most recent publication is the book and DVD, *Rhythmical Alchemy Playshop Volume 1, Drum Circle Games.*

You may contact him at:
arthurian@drumcircle.com
www.drumcircle.com

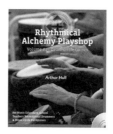

# NOTES

# NOTES

# NOTES

# NOTES

# NOTES

# NOTES

# NOTES